AND AGAIN
I HEARD
THE STARS

christie towers

Spuyten Duyvil
New York City

cover art by Kristine Roan

Library of Congress Cataloging-in-Publication Data

Names: Towers, Christie, author.
Title: And again I heard the stars / Christie Towers.
Description: New York City : Spuyten Duyvil, [2022] |
Identifiers: LCCN 2022003620 | ISBN 9781956005592 (paperback)
Subjects: LCGFT: Poetry.
Classification: LCC PS3620.O929 A85 2022 | DDC 811/.6--dc23/eng/20220225
LC record available at https://lccn.loc.gov/2022003620

CONTENTS

For now, and for centuries onwards

Song for Mary

And I heard a Heavenly voice speak

A star gave forth a multitude

To be perfected as much as she is able

My companion appeared

And she has been surrounded

A softness incomprehensible

The water gives testimony

In the dark night of their sins

The iron sits in the mouth

Proclaim and write thus

the octopus dreams a living light

Behold, the one sitting

A circle which resembled dawn

These two flowers bent a little

Show me the field of your soul

I want to leep over mountains and hills

Sickness is a hot fire to endure

I was not able to see any end to it

In your goodness please answer

But often I abandon them

Temporal kingdoms which rage within themselves

Into a wolf's mouth

Under the darker layer, there was the purest of air

O person, you are complete in every way

She is the expansion

A body and blood were brought forth

She had many eyes everywhere upon herself

A pricking of the flesh

We on earth

The image cried aloud

Bind yourself to the sweetness of god's love

Sometimes people can scarcely go on living

She will act as if a holy angel has commanded her

Behold the little place

Pour out thy heart like water

flame

hidden

tremble

hyacinth

vessel

terrible

miserable

star

Letter to Richardis (1)

Letter to Richardis (2)

Letter to Richardis (3)

Acknowledgements

Notes & Bibliography

FOR NOW, AND FOR CENTURIES ONWARDS
ANCRENE WISSE

fall to the earth bow or kneel keep
silence *for all souls departed* endure
the pains of prisoners fettered in misery
have pity mercy raise up god's body
out of the depths stand as you are able
out of terrible pain standing *my soul*
is narrow a small window *forget the*
world gleaming entirely out of body
I am here arising all broken *grant me*
to see your face brighter than the sun

SONG FOR MARY

O jewel resplendent O bright O
flood O sun that's flooded into you
abandon your husband abandon
O I have eagerly desired the purest
air a sapphire fountain the sweet
and tender shoot O where am I in exile
O living sun O fragile vessel I was to be
the companion of a closed gate a hidden
chamber I was to be the companion
of angels O where am I in rubied heavens
I had to descend breathless grieving I was
to be the companion I was to be the complaint
the soul living in the flesh O fragile flood
O vessel wondrously held hid within

And I heard a Heavenly voice speak

a reddish color a golden girdle
unutterable a lamb appears a golden
ray all brighter adorned a voice
speaks a color similar to the dawn
from her throat down to her uncovered
hyacinth she glowed she spoke to me
of darkness *I was thrown* into a language
a darkness *so horrible* and the light
white as a cloud from her navel
downward a hyacinth she had not yet
come into existence and again I heard
the stars and her voice like a hand *touched me*

A STAR GAVE FORTH A MULTITUDE

a great star embellished so
the sparks turned so the sparks
kindled all things turned sideways
rejecting god they did not think
about god a stranger only blazing
until burnt wood so the sparks
a loud whirlwind lifted from
corners leaned *in the direction*
of lost their inner beauty leaned
in the direction and lifted themselves
above destruction shining in brightness
they tended more they gulped they
tasted their own fall hurled backwards
exalted extinguished the sparks
turn a great star sideways

TO BE PERFECTED AS MUCH AS SHE IS ABLE

she is the ring the sweetest dawn
she shines an image clothed
in very white shoes a white veil
a woman *mouth open* she strains
she endures sweetly a holiness
the root of good a sword
unsheathed she held with great
devotion the dawn of the sun
without stain without burden of
human work a holiness her right
hand shining she is surrounded
hidden a little the depth of her
a sweetness a sword she held

My companion appeared

a red hyacinth an angel bright
as mirror two wings extended
a dove breathed into her ear
and I wanted I breathed the word
sweet and soft the word touches
the wound the left wing her
shoulder *I do not want to walk
with hypocrites* a serpent twisted
around a twig a pale color hanging
from her neck the truth *I want to be
green* wanted to gather it together
a green twig her two wings the dove
the ground trampled under foot
and I wanted *but I was not able* I
wanted to be green a serpent a twig
hanging twisted trampled under foot

AND SHE HAS BEEN SURROUNDED

as if in a mirror steeped with sun
pure intentions pant *a perfect work*
springs in them sighs and sighs
a pale-colored tunic a fountain
a dove *like a crystal* most keenly
glittered stretched as if ready turned
her lover looks away wings as if ready
for flying outstretched surrounded
her understanding a brighter burning
just as water leads she leads *just as*
a flying bird she spoke a pale confidence
a desire steadfast pants her lover looks
her hands in the air like water a fountain
she lifted up her eyes a flower outstretched

A SOFTNESS INCOMPREHENSIBLE

all earthly things declare
the mystery the terrible
goodness of her face *I was*
not able to see she was
in the form of a person
she was standing now
in the ashes of the flesh
a figure a garment a face
as if feathered all earthly
things running about their
desire uncovered their own
youthfulness burning various
and though the flower a figure
in the form of a person a face
a sweetness she carries as
terrible as lightning as grace

THE WATER GIVES TESTIMONY

before that light cast out
very pure from happiness
the soul passes a secret
breathing and the light
held within shines *sprang*
forth the perfect truth
the water the spirit hastens
for they are not whole
stirring in body crying
aloud they have been made
restored eternal *and the blood*
fruit-bearing in unity in unity the
water a rebirth a god who bloomed
in flesh lifted up again sprang
forth the word *through*
the water it grows and they
having been restored fell back
fulfilled with burning
tongues made light

In the dark night of their sins

I use a softer whip *for they know*
they burn they suffer in body they
have abandoned me altogether
their own flesh sweet rebellious
confined they wander burning they
delight they become withered in exile
they turn back *frightened at last* the
ancient serpent *the whip in god's hand*
a covenant a heaviness calling them

THE IRON SITS IN THE MOUTH
ANCRENE WISSE

turn away forbidden to eat *all this grief*
a look the root O feeble sister *it all comes*
of sight a sword's edge *the eyes* an arrow
feathered blinds the heart *open in god's*
name the veil your altar *keep silent* listen
dam up your words rise up towards heaven
the tongue wades in wetness slides easily
your hands raised your tongue bridled

PROCLAIM AND WRITE THUS

awake alert *with a clear mind*
in open places a burning light
just as the sun pours enkindled
inflamed my heart my breast its
rays a light coming continuous
I was a little girl I had passed
through a turning point a quiet
silence I was sick a long time
a silence a division of syllables
I refused to write I searched out
wished it to be manifest a voice
across the boundary speaking

THE OCTOPUS DREAMS A LIVING LIGHT

if she is dreaming do I dream with her
a change a color *her mantle flashing*
pale and dark one right after the other
a pattern *which signifies* an action
she sees a crab—a dramatic moment
she dreams herself *all dark* and like water
I follow *work diligently* roaming
when she leaves the bottom for a softer
scene *you could almost narrate the body*
a holiness a harmony perfect
no desire to rule over ardently
she swims sleeping to the shining surface
of the dream *you may wonder about these*
things but you are not strong enough *you plead*

Behold, the one sitting

indeed many sparkling rays
a lot of stars a soft shadow a
mountain *a very great brightness*
descending a voice crying
a sharp voice saying *extend*
yourself a wing of extraordinary
width *O you who are fragile*
crying aloud surrounded a bright
light obscure celestial a young
girl standing surrounded *this serenity*
an image filled with eyes indeed many
stars a lot of stars indeed many sparkling
rays *I was the one sitting upon*
that mountain a serenity soft a shadow

A CIRCLE WHICH RESEMBLED DAWN

she was standing close her hands
placed under her sleeves *she did not know*
he was standing in her heart her belly her breast
standing she was not touching the altar
her feet bloody-colored her hands placed under
breaking testament *god a great distance*
away a circle the circle of the earth the entire
circle the completion of her expansion her flesh
her heart an altar devoted to the rising
dawn a circle she came into

THESE TWO FLOWERS BENT A LITTLE

she held a vessel small bright this
vessel had a shine to it a flash of lightning
her face a certain brilliance many rays
divided from the clouds down to her breast
the light shone back her head uncovered
this beauty poured most brilliant I saw
the image brilliance out of brightness
her hair her shoes her tunic she stood
naked her entire body a lily and a rose
she was shaking a little she turned was
standing shaking the dust of ashes a body

Show me the field of your soul

O I am unworthy blameworthy
frail I frequently look for reasons
a righteous sign a fountain for I am
like ashes *I look more at the works*
of darkness the restraint of flesh
this burning perversity I am like
a tree flowering bowed down before
you flesh born from flesh I bless the
field *your heart* I sprout forth frail
fallen *turning my eyes around* I want
to communicate I carry my cross many
miseries O frailty *human nature shows itself*

I WANT TO LEEP OVER MOUNTAINS AND HILLS

the deer was ready running
the wind a true stone a blast
of wind the leaf of a tree flung
is stirred by the wind scattered
falling lower falling stirred on
the breast of the image a window
two stars standing separately
a wheel hanging in air an image
this person stood spoke stretched
just as a deer longs its hindfeet
upon the window the wheel building
itself spinning continuous *I want to look
back* a deer *so also my soul* sweet
transitory *I do not want to be*

SICKNESS IS A HOT FIRE TO ENDURE
ANCRENE WISSE

always for eternity *a bliss*
nothing cleanses sickness makes
a body understand what it is O
suffering child do not complain
prove patient your wound a greater
grace god's torments *look* your body
a shadow wretched weary *what does*
this messenger tell you to endure

I WAS NOT ABLE TO SEE ANY END TO IT

this great circle of gold color a
yellow cape an iron-colored stone
I was able to see a stone the color
of fire the flame is the flame a circle
so high above the earth *I could not*
comprehend the mist of darkness *the*
softness that dust has the fear hidden
in the stone *where I sit quaking* a person
living in time living as a stranger *I do not*
dare speak the brightness spread itself
the dawn glowing the color of steel
and fire the fire of the dove the same
one again spoke to me *as you have been*
taught speak now I will that you speak
a person of ashes a person O how
beautiful your eyes so full of story

In your goodness please answer

I was a child miserable more
than miserable unworthy very
concerned ignorant of all I speak
in womanly existence I ask you
to attend I was a child my tongue
could not express sometimes I
keep quiet confined sick unable
laid low I entreat you I speak as one
in doubt taught inwardly great
secrets I raise myself up I run I
speak a sweet power green a sacred
sound *things to be feared* a child
not a single hour a wanderer cast out
I ask you to attend seek all things
pass through the door in your soul
and know I wept I kept quiet a mystery

But often I abandon them

like I was the wind of a storm
a strong hand I strike and hurl
I strike them down I will not
speak I do not want to be found
they hurry they flee they do not
want to turn *no part of me* they hide
the flaming arrows their sins
swallowed into themselves *just*
as a worm goes they move *just as*
a worm into the earth they move
into death *no part of me*

TEMPORAL KINGDOMS WHICH RAGE WITHIN THEMSELVES

in the mouth of a wolf a rope
a wall smooth and bright a wall
of stone she appeared stretched
out *I could see her completely* her
thighs her knees her body down
to her ankles all bloody held
in the mouth a great jaw ironlike
and suddenly thunder *with such
force* a fog a woman shattered
shaking this woman appeared
gave forth a brightness a world
which is curved which is pressed
down weary of time temporal
kingdoms these fleshly desires
this wolf *tried to lift itself up*
behold the feet of a woman a
voice I heard *O let us turn back*

Into a wolf's mouth
Ancrene Wisse

if the spring goes muddy if the fiend
finds you if like a restive sheep you follow
turn away from the flock wander off
into bramble *the throat of hell* sister you
are the stone a tower consider your companions
confess your complaint endure a brightness
of vision your heart bends to temptation O
sister your flesh cries out a quiet strength

UNDER THE DARKER LAYER, THERE WAS THE PUREST OF AIR

blown by another turbulence
inside the circular object the gloomy
fire the outer edge a bright flame
a darker layer a very large globe
a reddish fire many clear spheres
everywhere and inside a shaking
so horrible full of sounds storms
a shaking *a fire so great* a darker
layer inside drew back to itself a
turbulence a great deal of thunder
spreading outward anticipated gave out
moisture a caressing rain *with softness*
inestimable gathered itself together
and again I heard and again a voice
gathered itself moved me

O PERSON, YOU ARE COMPLETE IN EVERY WAY

who does not know the hand
the very bright fire omnipotent
totally alive the movement of all
things no creature so dull so completely
hidden wretched creature incarnate
winged the fire inextinguishable
a fire wholly living all things bear
witness sighing the soul goes around
longing the spirit seeks a likeness a journey
behold the air a bolt of lightning not
transitory this flame rose up indivisible
blazing O person *just as the sky contains*
light a greenness in every direction
O little clod of earth *this flame breathed*
a power the dawn *gleamed through*

SHE IS THE EXPANSION

from the first planting a brilliance
embellished stretched out her secrets
naked a green seed hidden from me *hidden*
in the heart of god her head radiating holy
stretches upwards she dwells makes herself
like clouds a human body *I was not able*
to discern a ruddy faith her work open
the heart descended like lightning *this charity*
a green seed made flesh *I could not look*
and I saw *with such clear eyes* no person
no further likeness her hand upon her breast

A BODY AND BLOOD WERE BROUGHT FORTH

the flower hung down blazing
violently the wind the flame an airy
color very bright incomprehensible
the flame breathed this little clod
I am soft a fragile rib *I am a person*
not strong enough a body fell into
the bright fire a very dense darkness
increased a body *having been hurled*
became visible spoke aloud *O you*
who are miserable O tiny soul behold
the air inextinguishable *this flame*
sent forth a fire a secret inspiration

SHE HAD MANY EYES EVERYWHERE UPON HERSELF

she is terrified she trembles
she casts down she clings without
she exists she proceeds she is
restless she is without she holds
she totally refuses she had a bright
mirror she was shod with crystal
she restrains she has been crowned
she has the duty she bears these rules
she is surrounded she flees death
she does not have any courage she
trembles quaking in the hearts
of people her own complaint

A PRICKING OF THE FLESH
ANCRENE WISSE

in the hollow places my dove dear sister
hide yourself in clefts of rock flee to his wounds
beloved it lasts too long lift up your eyes
your heart like a shield give yourself come
boldly into laborious torment the first prickings
that sweet pleasure of discipline O sister
take your heart in your hand show it clearly

WE ON EARTH

will seek will always flee O woe wretched
fear of god who is able fearsome who will
help me unutterable I am not able to run
I want to go back O humility O virtues
it is impossible *you wished to trample me*
the newest day but *oh, oh, oh* most sweet
bud I was provoked scattered throughout
the world in great ruin *let all of us approach*
the most fruitfulness fleshly useless things

THE IMAGE CRIED ALOUD

I speak to them I surround I give
I want I become a beginning I warn
I want this to be understood I am
the grace I nurture I send work *I*
again warn I do not work wantonly
I despise these wounds I want to be
present I draw them together *I myself*
am a sinner I am not strong I do not
know I turn to I run for help I join myself
I hold them I considered their forms

Bind yourself to the sweetness of God's love

you will do these things a beginning
your whole soul all your mind you may
rise your flesh conquered your body
your whole heart your salvation you
will know *it will appear* the fear the
light of life this double work *her hands
and feet bound* obedient she trembled
the hyacinth made bright a human
nature the sweetness of god falling
one girdle over one shoulder falling
the same way your flesh conquered

Sometimes people can scarcely go on living

behold *I see inside* I will do
everything I will watch carefully
I demand that you restrain that
your conscience have the wounds
the sorrow I help you against
your worthlessness your flesh
your dwelling place inflamed I
suffered *you will hear an answer*
the earth agrees with me *you want*
to know things not known by flesh O
person this fruit the rain above
your heart *the sweat I demand from you*

She will act as if a holy angel has commanded her

with gentle words this book of quietness
a secret the end of the world a womb the last
day the land uncovered a limit *what will happen
then* the work completed the last day *I speak
within the scrolls* new secrets this human
person a rope *who brings together some mud*
like god in what way a fire of feebleness
a lion a beast a fiery dog truly a grisly wolf
the ancient serpent the most passionate burning

BEHOLD THE LITTLE PLACE

O you the root the first material
the leaping fountain the bright
flower *who wanted to fly upward*
untouched a heart which breathes
O behold a living angel destroyed
plunged into ruin the ancient heart
the little place *which alone flowered*

POUR OUT THY HEART LIKE WATER
ANCRENE WISSE

if the dust of light searched all corners
the heart wrung out within ourselves
the throat of hell the lost word a fire sister
you must confess *I spoke I watched I touched
my hand* nakedly speak uncover a turbulence
the depth one wades a wound weeping a ruddy
shame more horrible still torn to pieces
a dead color become beautiful red water

FLAME

a hot glowing generated to ignite
provoked swollen or intensified red
luminosity a strong feeling a quickening
arousal a source of illumination a quality
cloudless and reflective *a vital energy*
a fervent passion combustive robust
conspicuous a euphemism for hell
for power a desire alight in ashes animate
a signal sudden the dawn a swift transfer
of information that by which we see
a celestial body pale in color electric
reaching out a pathway known a particular
aspect a set of principles O small burden

HIDDEN

in the mountains from the eyes
of all living sheltered a silence which
pervades the being the body remote
very far away held within the cover
I kept my mouth closed hands open
obscure emblems of light a seclusion
the mountains covered my body unbearable
bound O burning the image held me in its hand

TREMBLE

in frailty or excitement a leaf
in the wind a flicker of flame a
lip before speaking to quake
involuntarily a fit or spell of
quivering that which holds
arrows that which betrays
fear an anxiety which moves
the body like a weapon a small
animal a convulsive shiver which
halts which moves irregularly to
clasp hands to pray a body entire

HYACINTH

a flower or stone an opening
its origins in fire *place it over*
the eyes slick with saliva for
anyone bewitched suffering
pains of the heart a dense cluster
of blooms bell-shaped compact
spikes precious stone of the
ancients to guard against lightning
melancholy a bird of massive size
may he release you from all pain

VESSEL

body as boat container a cask
which holds some true quality
buoyant steerable put in place
for use to engage in service
the embodiment an exhibition
of emptiness holy a state of
transfer a longing sent forth
a place where grace may enter
mouths open hands we embark
empty our bodies out to sea

TERRIBLE

in difficult awe exciting
or extreme alarm an intense
fear a dread which bears
reluctance an apprehension
to approach we are wooden
ships engulfed with flame
we row wearily the sea the
rocky shore boulders before
us our bodies built to tremble
before the unknown a power
incomprehensible a voice
which calls us forward
halting to hurry we heave

MISERABLE

pitiably small O wretched soul
lonely obscure shut off from the
light O gloomy ember sunless
suffering to stay lit you dwell
in darkness of doubt a shroud
of suffering O small flame casting
shadows listen for your name

STAR

a body visible expanding
the bearer of light luminous
ornament a sign in darkness
a small thing outstanding against
a drape of night a small thing
falling piteously rising a wanderer
on a raging sea foaming lost for ever

Letter to Richardis (1)

no one knows for sure your body
O tender shoot young as I used to be
your body 900 years after us eager
on screen kneeling at my feet you say
you only want to be anywhere I am
the gravel rolls unsteady the camera
closes in your small mouth *a sacrament*
in itself and no one knows for sure *the breath*
that passed between us knees bent hair
uncovered we knelt we worshipped a body

LETTER TO RICHARDIS (2)

they imagine your mouth an animal
hungry twitching *I want to subordinate myself
to you* obedient creature a voice like water I wade
tread slow seek the tide of each eye deep water
surrounds me and we are standing in a room
of stone and you ask again *will you take me*

Letter to Richardis (3)

listen O sister I speak to you
in spirit my grief a narrow bird flies
up to heaven my grief destroys all consolation
O why have you forsaken me an orphan
in your absence feeble a sinner I mistake
the sun for god I look for you O creature
of light I wither desolate my heart snatched
from its chamber O love listen *remember me*

Acknowledgements

Bedfellows.   "Letter to Richardis (1)"
                   "Letter to Richardis (2)"
                   "Letter to Richardis (3)"

Infinite thanks to Hildegard, for her spiritual companionship and guidance. Thank you for teaching me to listen to and trust in the spirit, for helping me to see the divinity of our bodies, our love, and the endlessly surprising and sacred beauty of creation.

Great, heartfelt gratitude to Jill McDonough and my Documentary Poetics cohort at UMass Boston for receiving and believing in these poems. Thank you for teaching me to write and live fearlessly. Without you, these poems and this person would have never found their way.

Thank you to Lillian-Yvonne Bertram, for teaching me to delight in experimental poetics. Thank you to Lindsey Warren for believing in this manuscript. Special thanks to Kate Glavin, James Parker, Megan Waring, Eliza Jerrett, Todd Perry, and Carolyn Kepes for your friendship and guidance as these poems came into being. Thank you for all the late nights, long talks and walks. Thank you for holding my wild heart.

Finally, thank you to the editors of Spuyten Duyvil for loving this book into physical form.

NOTES & BIBLIOGRAPHY

Bibliography with specific editions and translations for each source follows the Notes.

For now, and for centuries onwards, The iron sits in the mouth, Sickness is a hot fire to endure, Into a wolf's mouth, A pricking of the flesh, and *Pour out thy heart like water* are distillations of chapters, or parts of chapters, and use words and phrases from the *Ancrene Wisse.*

flame, hidden, tremble, hyacinth, vessel, terrible, miserable, and *star* were generated, in part, with inspiration from the Merriam-Webster Dictionary Online. *hyacinth* uses text from Hildegard von Bingen's *Physica.*

Song for Mary borrows words and phrases from Hildegard von Bingen's *Symphonia,* particularly the "Antiphons for The Virgin". Some words and phrases borrowed from an online archive full text of *Hildegard of Bingen: Selected Writings.*

https://archive.org/stream/SelectedWritingsHildegardOfBingenMarkAtherton/Selected%20Writings%20-%20Hildegard%20of%20Bingen%20%26%20Mark%20Atherton_djvu.txt

the octopus dreams a living light uses words and phrases from *Mystical Visions,* pages 324-325. as well as text and transcriptions of dialogue from this online article and embedded video:
https://www.newsweek.com/octopus-color-sleeping-dreaming-scientist-1461314

In your goodness please answer uses text from Hildegard's "Letter to Bernard of Clairvaux" from the *Selected Writings.*

Letter to Richardis (1), Letter to Richardis (2), and *Letter to Richardis (3)* are inspired by and referring to and use translated dialogue from *Vision,* the 2010 film about the life of Hildegard. *Letter to Richardis (3)* uses some text from Hildegard's final letter to Richardis as printed in *Hildegard of Bingen: The Woman of Her Age.*

All other poems use words and phrases from Hildegard von Bingen's *Mystical Visions.*

Atherton, Mark, and Hildegard. *Full Text of "Selected Writings St Hildegard Of Bingen"*,
    archive.org/stream/SelectedWritingsHildegardOfBingenMarkAtherton/
    Selected%20Writings%20-%20Hildegard%20of%20Bingen%20%26%20Mark%20
    Atherton_djvu.txt.

Cahill, Thomas. *Mysteries of the Middle Ages: and the Beginning of the Modern World.*
    Anchor Books, 2008.

Fox, Matthew, and Hildegard. *Hildegard Von Bingen's Mystical Visions.* Bear & Company,
    1986.

Georgiou, Aristos. "Octopus That Changes Color While Sleeping Might Be Dreaming,
    Scientist Says." *Newsweek*, Newsweek, 27 Sept. 2019, www.newsweek.com/
    octopus-color-sleeping-dreaming-scientist-1461314.

Hildegard, and Barbara Newman. *Symphonia: a Critical Edition of the Symphonia Armonie
    Celestium Revelationum.* Cornell University Press, 1998.

Hildegard, and Mark Atherton. *Selected Writings.* Penguin, 2001.

Hildegard, and Priscilla Throop. *Hildegard Von Bingen's Physica: The Complete English
    Translation of Her Classic Work on Health and Healing.* Healing Arts Press, 1998.

Maddocks, Fiona. *Hildegard of Bingen: The Woman of Her Age.* Faber and Faber, 2013.

Von Trotta, Margarethe, director. *Vision.* Zeitgeist Films, 2010.

White, Hugh. *Ancrene Wisse: Guide for Anchoresses.* Penguin Books Ltd, 2001.

CHRISTIE TOWERS is a poet living in Somerville, MA. She holds an MFA in poetry from the University of Massachusetts, Boston and is currently pursuing an M.Div at Boston University's School of Theology. This is her first collection.

www.ingramcontent.com/pod-product-compliance
Lightning Source LLC
Chambersburg PA
CBHW011218120626
46545CB00008B/3052